89

DATE DUE

JAN 2 1983			
MAY 3 1 1983			
JUL 1 4 1983			
FEB 6 1986			
MAR 7 1988			
SEP 2 0 1991			
MAR 2 1 1992			
JUN 3 0 1992			
SEP 3 - 1996			
261-2500		Printed in USA	

BIOLOGICAL
CLOCKS

BIOLOGICAL

CLOCKS

SARAH R. RIEDMAN

ILLUSTRATED BY
LESLIE MORRILL

THOMAS Y. CROWELL

NEW YORK

Library of Congress Cataloging in Publication Data

Riedman, Sarah Regal, 1902–
  Biological clocks.
  Bibliography: p.
  Includes index.
  Summary: Describes the inbuilt mechanism that
regulates the rhythms of life in all living things and
discusses how these rhythms are set and what happens
when they become distorted.
  1. Biological rhythms—Juvenile literature.
[1. Biological rhythms] I. Morrill, Leslie, ill.
II. Title.
QH527.R53   574.1'882   81–43873
ISBN 0–690–04182–9
ISBN 0–690–04183–7 (lib. bdg.)   AACR2

1 2 3 4 5 6 7 8 9 10
First Edition

ACKNOWLEDGMENTS

The author is deeply indebted to Mr. George S. Fichter, entomologist, naturalist, and unimaginably versatile author, for his review of the manuscript. His generous help in checking factual accuracy in the many areas of his competence, and his editorial comments and suggested changes have done much to smooth out rough edges here and there. For all this, everlasting gratitude.

S.R.R.

CONTENTS

1

WE

LIVE

BY

RHYTHMS

AS YOU AWAKEN, open your eyes, stretch, and jump out of bed, a series of changes is started inside your body. Chemicals, called steroids, flow from glands, rush into the bloodstream, and prepare you for daytime activities. Your heartbeat increases and breathing becomes faster as you wash, dress, eat breakfast, and get ready for school.

Throughout the day other body changes happen. Your temperature rises gradually to about 1° F higher in the late afternoon. Blood pressure, lowest during the early hours of the morning, peaks in early evening. Later you become sleepy and during the night, both heartbeat and temperature decrease until they return to the morning level. Invisible "clocks" inside us govern this daily rhythm of wakefulness and sleep, of work and rest.

Other rhythms are set on a three- or four-hour schedule. When you feel hungry, it's because stomach contractions "tell" you that you need food. At certain periods during the day you are full of energy, and at others dull and sluggish; you feel happy or moody, friendly or lonely. You go from alertness to daydreaming. These feelings show up in your ability to solve problems, in test scores, and in strength of handgrip.

Other living things besides humans have clocks that help determine their activities. In sunlight, green plants unfold their leaves and manufacture food; darkness sets the time for the leaves to droop in rest.

At dawn, the rooster crows and the bird in the tree chirps. While both go to roost at nightfall, the clocks of the owl and bat are set for rising then. Sea animals follow an equally regular, twice-daily rhythm of the ocean tides. The oyster opens its shell at high tide, which brings the sea creatures it eats. As the tide goes out the oyster shuts its shell tight.

The rhythms of all living things are linked to the rhythms of the earth and its satellite, the moon. As the earth turns on its axis we get day and night, light and darkness. As the earth whirls in its yearly cycle around the sun, we get the seasons: summer and win-

Rooster at daybreak

Rooster at nightfall

ter, spring and fall. The moon's gravitational pull on the earth causes the ebb and flow of the ocean tides.

The rhythms of plants and animals, including humans, have been named according to the earth's motions, from which living things took the cues to set their living clocks.

Circadian, the daytime/nighttime 24-hour cycle, gets its name from the Latin words *circa* meaning "about" and *dies,* meaning "day." The sparrow and gray squirrel, diurnal or daytime-active animals, as well as the owl and bat, nocturnal or nighttime-active animals, alternate their periods of activity and rest in circadian rhythm.

Tidal is the rhythm of marine animals. This is timed by the twice-daily tides of the moon in a cycle of 24.8 hours.

The moon's twice-monthly cycle from crescent to full to its waning phase brings the very high and very low tides. This is called the *lunar* rhythm and occurs in a 28-day cycle. Sea animals' clocks time their breeding by this cycle.

Circannual rhythms are rhythms "around the year." They govern the seasonal activities of animals during reproduction, hibernation, and migration as well as plants' seasonal flowering, seed production, and sprouting.

Ultradian are rhythms at short intervals: in cycles of about 90 minutes in sleep in animals and in humans, and in the daytime when people have changes of mood or energy level.

Scientists tell us that plants and animals have adapted to the earth's rhythms from the beginning of life on the planet. Each generation of plant and animal starts its life inheriting the rhythmic patterns of its ancestors. Each animal is born with its own species' type of rhythm. Chicks newly hatched in incubators, without the mother hen, feed by light in the brooder and sleep when the lights are turned out. Human babies come into the world with a sleep-wake cycle. Even while in the mother's body, the unborn baby kicks and moves during periods of activity and remains quiet at other times.

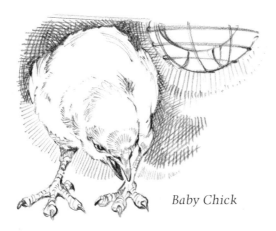

Baby Chick

A few scientists do not agree that biological rhythms of living things are self-timed. They deny the existence of internal living clocks. They say that light, gravity, temperature changes, air pressure, and radiation from space directly set the rhythms. But by far the great majority of scientists are firm in the idea of inner living clocks.

While unusual happenings may temporarily upset a normal rhythm, it is not lost. An eclipse of the sun will confuse birds. The sudden darkness momentarily disrupts their timekeeping. They become restless because they do not know whether to roost at what seems to be the wrong time. Yet it has been found that some plants left in the dark in a cave continue for several days to open and close their leaves.

Chronobiology is a new branch of biology that deals with these biological rhythms. Its name is taken from the Greek *chronos,* meaning "time," and was chosen to show the importance of time in ordering life processes. Today, in chronobiology laboratories at universities and medical centers, researchers are studying the rhythms of plants, animals, and people.

This book deals with these rhythms. It will tell how each plant flowers at a special month, even at a different time of day; how insects are timed for their active and resting stages of development; how some sea worms breed only during a specific phase of the moon during two fall months; when birds molt, build nests, and migrate; how some animals hibernate or change their fur coats with the seasons; about the migrations, mating, and feeding of whales.

It will also tell how the rhythms inside our bodies occur in sleep and during waking hours. Read on to find out how these living clocks inside us set the times when we are most alert for learning, playing, scoring, and what happens when the rhythms are distorted and the clocks need to be reset.

2

PLANTS

HAVE

CLOCKS

AND

CALENDARS

SNOW IS STILL on the ground and the forest trees are leafless in Vermont and upstate New York when the sap begins running in the sugar maples. For the farmer spring has arrived and it's sapping time. He hangs the buckets on the tree trunks to collect the sugary sap, which he will boil down to maple syrup.

On the forest floor skunk cabbages poke their foul-smelling broad leaves through the melting snow. For these plants spring also comes early. It will be another month by the plant calendar before the delicate purplish hepatica flowers show. Still, they will be in time to catch the sun before the awakening leaves on the trees shut out the sunlight. Each kind of flower has its own time to bloom.

Later, and long before the calendar reads June 21, the first day of summer, trees burst with tiny leaves that had been tucked away in leaf buds during the previous year. Then the trees will fully unfold their fresh, green leaves. After a long winter sleep the leaves turn to the sun to capture its rays and begin manufacturing food.

Flowering trees, each at its own time, reveal colorful blossoms. In the summer, fruit will form from the blossoms. From the fruit, nut, and cone will come seeds later in the season. Each sprouting seed will grow into a seedling capable of starting a new tree.

As autumn approaches, the days get shorter and the nights grow longer and cooler; the tree sap stops flowing. Some trees display their fall colors of orange, golden brown, blue-purple, and scarlet red. These splashy colors signal the sure death of the leaves. They begin to fade, turn dry, drop off, and litter the forest floor. The trees' winter rest starts, and they stand bare of foliage. It is the end of another year's cycle, of winter sleep or dormancy, spring awakening, active summer growth, and autumn fading.

How are these seasonal events timed to happen on schedule each year? Plants set their biological clocks for growth and flowering by the amount of light they get during a day. How long is a day? Is it 8, 10, or

14 hours from sunup to sundown? It depends on the season. The daily newspaper for the first day of spring prints: "Sunrise Today 6:24 A.M.; Sunset Today 6:32 P.M." On this day there is daylight for 12 hours and 8 minutes. The days grow longer from spring to summer, and shorter from fall to winter. In the Northern Hemisphere June 21 is the longest day and December 22 the shortest day of the year. The reverse is true in the Southern Hemisphere.

The length of day that signals blossoming time differs from plant to plant. Some need a short day to flower, others a long day. Botanists call the day length requirement of a plant its photoperiod.

In your yard, crocus is the first flower to appear, announcing spring when the sun is still low in the sky. Black-eyed susan, gladiolus, and clover appear later. Cherry blossoms open around Easter time; orange and grapefruit in Florida bloom during the first days of March. In the same backyard, mango trees are already in bloom in February.

Chrysanthemums and poinsettias are short-day flowers, as are asters, dahlias, and violets. These produce blooms in early spring or fall, when there is less than 12 hours of daylight. Delphinium and larkspur are long-day flowers, blooming in early summer when there is light for longer than 12 hours. Carnations, dandelions, and snapdragons bloom at any day length and are called day-neutral.

Crocus
Dandelion
Clover

THE "FLOWER CLOCK"

Even flowers that blossom in the same season may open and close at different *hours* of the day. Carolus Linnaeus, the eighteenth-century botanist, was the first to recognize this. He even made up a "flower clock," one flower for each hour, representing the face of a clock.

6 A.M.	SPOTTED CAT'S-EAR OPENS
7 A.M.	AFRICAN MARIGOLD OPENS
8 A.M.	MOUSE-EAR HAWKWEED OPENS
9 A.M.	PRICKLY SOW THISTLE CLOSES
10 A.M.	COMMON NIPPLEWORT CLOSES
11 A.M.	STAR OF BETHLEHEM OPENS
12 noon	PASSIONFLOWER OPENS
1 P.M.	CHILDING PINK CLOSES
2 P.M.	SCARLET PIMPERNEL CLOSES
3 P.M.	HAWKBIT CLOSES
4 P.M.	SMALL BINDWEED CLOSES
5 P.M.	WHITE WATER LILY CLOSES
6 P.M.	EVENING PRIMROSE OPENS

Linnaeus's clock was so accurate that Europeans for years afterward planted flower beds in the shape of a clock, each bed blossoming at its own hour. On a sunny day, they could tell the time just by looking in the garden.

FLOWERING TO ORDER

Knowing from experience the photoperiod of a particular plant, flower growers can control its time of flowering to suit their seasonal needs. By changing the length of day artificially, with lights on in the greenhouse for the plant's photoperiod, they can be sure to have chrysanthemums for Thanksgiving and poinsettias for Christmas. What's more, they can produce two crops of chrysanthemums, one for Christmas and one for Easter. Here is how the grower does it.

In December and January he shines lights on the chrysanthemum seedlings at night. This stimulates their growth: the stems grow tall, the leaves numerous. The continuous light, however, delays the flowering. Then in March, while the days are still short, he turns lights off, and the chrysanthemums—now tall-stemmed—quickly produce flowers in time for Easter.

VEGETABLES IN SEASON

What about the photoperiods of vegetables? Spinach and lettuce are long-day plants, maturing in summer.

String beans and tomatoes ripen at any day length; they are day-neutral. What happens when the vegetable seeds of a plant with a known photoperiod are planted at the "wrong" time? An experiment with the Biloxi soybean, a short-day plant, gave the answer. Seeds were planted at three different times: one group early in spring, another batch in June, and another in July. All plants bloomed in September—the season for their flowering. But what a difference turned up in the crop! Those planted in the spring were five feet tall; the other two groups were dwarfed, the ones planted in July being the shortest. All three had met their timetable for blooming in September, but those planted late missed out on full growth.

RAINS START THE CLOCKS FOR DESERT FLOWERS

Short and long days alone don't make flowers bloom. For example, in the California Mojave desert, the land is sunbaked dry most of the year. Under a cloudless sky the daytime temperature is scorchingly high. At night the desert turns cold, as the heat of the day escapes into the upper air. For much of the year there is little sign of life, except for cactus and other plants that have developed ways of storing water.

But when the rains come, the desert springs to life almost overnight. As if by magic, brilliantly colored flowers erupt. For only a couple of weeks the desert

Desert Flowers

is a luscious garden of rare beauty. Desert flowers are timed to be in a hurry if they are to produce seeds before the desert is once more dry.

The same rains that bring the flowers also awaken the many insects in the desert. They too have a timetable. Emerging as adults in the final stage of their development, flies, beetles, bees, moths, and butterflies coming out of dormancy make the most of the few weeks to catch pollen or nectar. A hasty visit to a flower brings the reward. For the flower, receiving an insect is all important for fertilization. It will insure a crop of seeds for next year.

Some desert flowers bloom only in the morning and evening hours, because the midday heat and sun evaporate the nectar. The evening primrose opens its rosette of flowers at dusk. The white or pale yellow flowers

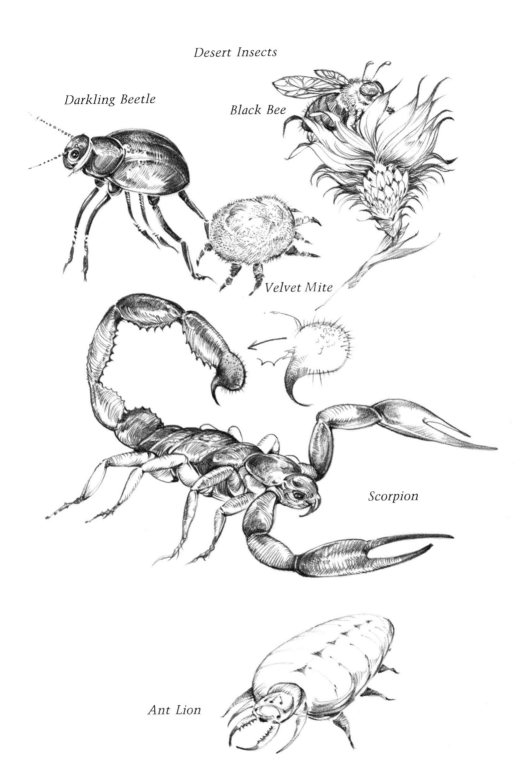

Desert Insects

Darkling Beetle

Black Bee

Velvet Mite

Scorpion

Ant Lion

Desert Flowers

are still visible to moths then. Columbines and verbenas attract bees during the day with their showy blue and yellow petals. These colors are most visible to bees. Indian paint-brush and many lilies in bright red and orange entice butterflies, which are active in the daytime. It's as if the clocks of flowers were "synchronized" with those of particular insects, the way people synchronize their watches to meet at a certain time.

In the short desert cycle, pollen is transferred, flowers are fertilized, seeds are formed, and the blooms fade away. The seeds sink into the ground; it is time for them to sleep until the next rainy season. They too have timetables. In the Arizona desert there are two rainy seasons. Some flowers bloom with the summer rains, others only in the winter rainy season. The seeds of summer flowers, though soaked by winter rains, will not sprout; and the seeds of winter flowers will lie dormant under summer showers.

FLOWERING ELSEWHERE
ON THE GLOBE

In temperate climates the growing season is much
longer than in the desert. The amount of light varies
during the day and suits the photoperiods of different
flowers. And so there are different flowers in different
seasons.

In the tropics, day and night are of equal length.
And so flowers may bloom several times during the
year.

In arctic lands such as Siberia and in parts of Alaska,
there is a long season of nighttime darkness in winter
and a two-month-long summer when the sun doesn't
set at all. But during the brief summer the blades of
grass break through the thawing layer of permafrost.
Buried seeds sprout, and wild flowers of many colors
cover the ground. During that time, flies and mosquitoes, especially large and numerous, flourish.

With the first hint of winter in August, the insects
disappear and the flowers die leaving behind the seeds
in the frozen ground. In these parts of the globe, the
day length of nearly 24 hours sets the flowering schedule for the plant clocks.

3

TIMED

WITH

THE

TIDES

ANIMALS LIVE BY rhythms just as plants do. Those that make their homes in the ocean or at its edge clock their feeding and resting times with the daily tides. And they breed in time with the moon's phases, which occur twice a month, during the lunar cycle. At full moon the tide, known as the *spring tide,* is unusually high. During the one-quarter and three-quarter phases of the moon, the *neap tide* is unusually slight.

The sea pansy resembles a flower on a short stalk and belongs to the same family as jellyfish and sea anemones. Like them, it has tentacles or "arms," with which it reaches out to capture food. At night a sea pansy glows with a cold light, like a firefly or lightning bug. At this time it is actively feeding. As the tide rises, it thrusts its tentacles upward in the water to catch tiny bits of floating or swimming food: diatoms, fish larvae, copepods. When the tide is out, it withdraws its tentacles and remains hidden in the sand. Thus, it follows the circadian rhythm in a 24-hour cycle. In the breeding season and during high tide, sea pansies release many swimming larvae, each capable of developing into a colony. The life cycle of the sea pansy is then complete.

The sand hopper, or beach flea, is an agile little shrimplike creature. When searching for food sand hoppers head for the water's edge in droves just ahead of the tide. During these nightly migrations, they get their fill of decaying seaweed and bits of dead animals washed up on shore. At sunrise they leave the feeding area and bury themselves in sand burrows they dig each morning.

Once a biologist transported some sand hoppers during the night from the western shore of Italy clear across the peninsula and released them on the Adriatic shore in the morning. Instead of heading for the water's edge, they turned around hopping overland in the direction from which they came. It was daytime, and by their inner clocks it was time to hasten to their burrows.

Not all sea inhabitants can swim or hop on the beach.

Oysters, clams, and mussels cannot reach for food with tentacles. They live inside a hard shell and are bound to a rock for life, tied down by a structure called a byssus. It is made of a mass of horny threads secreted by the byssus gland. Since they can't move they have to depend on the rhythm of the tides for food. At high tide, oysters open their shells and filter out whatever food the rising water brings. As the tide goes out, the shell is shut tight, protecting the animal from the sun and air.

So fixed is their life to the tides that when flown to land inside a tank of water they continue to open their shells at the time the tide is high in their previous watery home. Here is an experiment that proved this.

Oysters were flown in lightproof containers from an East Coast fishery to a laboratory in Illinois, 1,000 miles from their home. For about two weeks the oysters continued to open their shells at the time of the Connecticut high tides. Only much later did the rhythm of shell opening and closing drift out of the phase of the tides. The oysters had by then reset their clocks to the moon's cycle by Illinois time. (You will remember that the tides are caused by the gravitational pull of the moon.)

The breeding of oysters is timed by the lunar month. At full moon with the spring tide oysters spawn, shedding millions of egg and sperm cells, which unite in the sea. The fertilized eggs hatch into free-swimming larvae. After a while each larva sinks to the bottom, forms a tiny shell, and attaches itself to some solid object. At this stage it is known as a spat, and unless it finds a suitable support it dies. Once fixed in position it goes on to develop into an adult oyster.

ONE STILL TIED TO THE SEA

Other creatures have left the sea, but cannot live their full life on land. A ghost crab spends at least three-fourths of its busy life on land, but visits the ocean for some of its needs. It has not completely cut itself off from the sea where its ancestors lived millions of years ago.

At night the ghost crab races over the beach. The speediest of all crabs, its nickname is rabbit of crustaceans, or sharp-footed one. But why ghost? During the day it may suddenly pop up on the beach, because it does not feed in the sea. Just as promptly it disappears before you notice where it came from and where it went. Since it matches the color of the sand so perfectly, it need only squat to become invisible. On a moonlit night it can stand still casting a shadow for just a moment.

Night is the ghost crab's time to feed. Without getting its feet wet it waits at the water's edge for bits of food. When the tide is out, it finds small beached

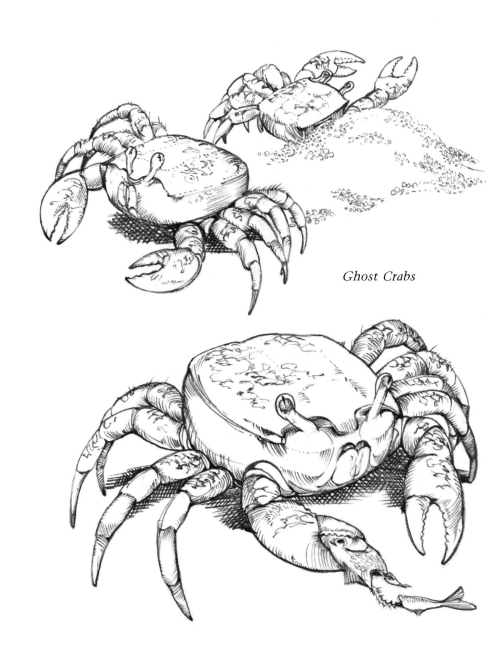

Ghost Crabs

fish or refuse washed in from a passing ship. It also feeds on any careless sand fleas or tiny mole crabs that happen to wander past.

Casting about all night for food, crabs return at dawn to their burrows in U-shaped and Y-shaped tunnels dug high on the beach. Then, before the sun is high, they mend and enlarge their burrows. By midday they have plugged the tunnel entrances. Safe inside from enemies such as seagulls or larger crabs, they also escape the drying sun. Inside the burrow the crabs remain asleep until feeding time at night.

Not completely adapted to life on land, ghost crabs must from time to time go to the water's edge to wet their gills to get air. Since ghost crabs do not have lungs they cannot breathe air. They get oxygen when the water runs through their gills.

They also show their attachment to the sea at spawning time. Most of the summer the female crab carries her eggs and supplies them with oxygen from her body. At intervals she wades into the ocean hugging the eggs under her abdomen while a wave passes over. Only then does she shake the eggs loose from special appendages called swimmerets. The eggs hatch into larvae, which spend their infancy in the water. Eventually, they leave the water and dig holes on the beach. There, safe from the waves, they change into the adult crab form.

Spawning, like reproduction in many other animals,

is seasonal. For the ghost crab it occurs in the warm months. Another seasonal event is hibernation. At the end of the summer, ghost crabs move up high on the beach above the watermark. There they build tunnels deep enough to avoid the cold. Until the next spring they remain in the tunnels in a dormant state without feeding.

In its life on land and only briefly going to the water for specific needs, a ghost crab follows three rhythms: feeding at low tide (tidal rhythm of 24.8 hours); resting in burrows on circadian rhythm (24-hour cycle); and breeding and hibernating on circannual or seasonal rhythm.

Another species of crab that burrows on shore and feeds at night is the fiddler crab. However, it differs from the ghost crab in that it changes color on the solar cycle. But first, how did it get its name?

The male fiddler crab has one very much enlarged claw. When the claw is held across the front or raised and waved, it reminds people of a violin bow. The fiddler uses its "bow" to feed, to attract the female, to defend itself against an attacker, or to threaten an intruder.

Fiddler crabs construct their burrows on shore where they can't be inundated by the flow, or high, tide. At ebb, or low, tide they leave the burrows to search for food. But exactly every 12 hours they go through a color change. At night they turn pale. This is a camouflage against prowling raccoon or other enemies. In

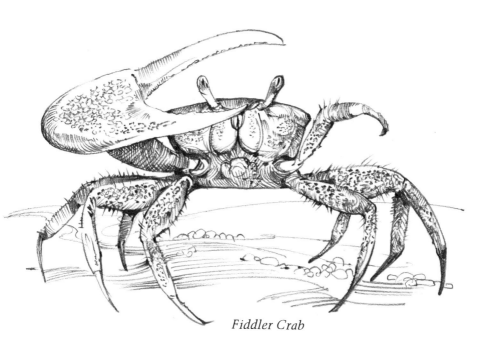

Fiddler Crab

the daytime they take on the dark color, which protects them from the sun's rays.

The skin below the fiddler's semitransparent shell contains pigment granules. The fiddler crab changes from light to dark by alternately spreading and clumping these pigment granules, a rhythm that has intrigued biologists.

In a laboratory tank, the fiddler continues to change its color, without time cues of light and dark, or of high and low tides. This change follows the circadian cycle. The crab runs around in the tank and feeds on what would be a 24.8-hour tidal rhythm as if it were on the seashore. Its inner clock times these activities with remarkable regularity. One researcher found that the students working in his laboratory planned a trip to the crab's home by following the crab's patterns recorded on charts, rather than official tide tables.

WORM DANCE TO
THE QUARTER MOON

At sunrise during the last quarter of the moon in October and November, the Samoan palolo worm puts on a spectacular swarming performance. The native people of the Samoa and Fiji islands in the South Pacific await this annual event, which they call the great rising.

The palolo worms live among rock in coral reefs where they forage for food. All year long they prepare for swarming by adding many foot-long pieces at the hind end. Timed exactly to the waning moon in the southern spring (October and November), the worms rise to the surface to reproduce. The islanders familiar with the worms' rhythm are there for the happening. The worms' segments break off and go through a whirling breeding dance, churning the water into a froth.

The islanders quickly scoop up as much as they can carry off of the worms' pieces and roast them into a tasty dish. Then the remaining segments in the water explode and release eggs and sperm from female and male worms. Sperm find eggs, and fertilization is accomplished. In circannual rhythm the worms have fulfilled their destined function to breed.

Not only intertidal and shore inhabitants, but many bottom fish come to the surface to spawn in season. Their eggs, sperm, larvae, and young mingle as part of the plankton, the floating mixture of living things.

But the grunion, a slender, silvery food fish, is one of several fish that deliberately abandons the water to deposit its eggs for safekeeping elsewhere.

The grunion spawns from March to August immediately after the full moon. The female waits until the tide passes its flood stage, slackens, and begins to ebb. At that exact moment, she leaves the water, buries her tail in the beach's sand, and there lays her eggs. The nearest male sheds his sperm on the eggs. The timing is most important: the eggs need to be fertilized on the ebb tide. Why? If the female were to deposit them on the flood tide, they would be washed out to sea before they could be fertilized.

And so even the most primitive creatures breed and protect themselves—adults and young—by setting their inner clocks to the rhythms of the earth and moon.

4
INSECTS
CAN
''TELL''
TIME

INSECTS ARE EVERYWHERE, even in frozen Antarctica. Insects make up the largest group of animals with about 1 million species known today. Those that destroy crops, carry disease to cattle and people, kill trees, damage buildings, chew holes in woolen clothing, and infest foods are considered man's enemies. Many of the rest are our helpers. Some pollinate flowers necessary for growing fruits and vegetables. Insects that eat other insects, such as the ladybird beetle, or ladybug, which feeds on aphids, save many trees. Others are food for many larger animals: frogs and salamanders, bats, birds, and anteaters.

Insects develop from egg to adult in different ways. Most pass through four stages: (1) egg; (2) larva, an actively feeding form; (3) pupa, or cocoon, a resting stage; to (4) adult. These stages follow each other, timed by clocks that are cued by the length of day. And day length, of course, changes with the seasons.

INSECTS IN SEASON

With the coming of spring and longer periods of daylight, biological clocks stir the creatures out of their winter sleep in pupal cases. They emerge from the cases and change into adults. Soon adult insects lay eggs that hatch into larvae, in time to devour unfolding leaves and budding flowers on fruit trees.

As the days shorten, at the end of August, the well-fed larvae spin silky cases around themselves for protection during the winter. Though many changes occur inside the cocoon during the cold months, outwardly this is an insect rest period called diapause.

Each insect species has its own "right" time to retire for the winter, to emerge in the spring, and, as adults, to lay eggs. Agricultural scientists have found that just as the biological clocks of plants set the time for growth and flowering, insect clocks of different species set the time for larvae to eat, and for pupal diapause.

In a laboratory, a scientist shone a light on silkworm

cocoons continuously for 16 hours. Under this light, equal to a summer's day length, the pupae were awakening, ending their developing stage in the dead of winter. Other cocoons of the same species exposed to light for only 8 hours (to mimic a winter day) did not end their diapause. Knowing a particular insect's timing, a farmer or fruit grower can control or interfere with its development.

BUSY AT NIGHT

Unlike flies and butterflies, which are active in the daytime, moths, crickets, and cockroaches are up during the night. The cave cricket is not only nocturnal but doubly so, for it never sees daylight. Still, its clock tells the cricket when it is time to leave the darkness of the cave to forage in the darkness of night. On a true circadian rhythm it feeds at night and returns before dawn to rest in the cave.

Cockroaches are unwelcome guests to kitchens and cellars. During the day they disappear into dark corners and sheltered cracks, around pipes, and behind loose baseboards. At night they come out to eat. If you put a light on at night you see them scurrying to their hiding places. Their feeding time has been interrupted!

Several kinds of ants can be said to work on a night shift too, earning their living by tending aphids. Aphids pierce the stems, leaves, and buds of plants with needle-sharp stylets in their beaks and suck the sap. They excrete a sticky, sweet substance, known as honeydew, which is the ants' food. At night the ants carry off the aphids to their nests below ground for protection; in return they get a sweet meal. The next morning the ants take the aphids on a trip to another juicy plant. While the aphids go to work sucking sap, the ants are back in their underground nests, well fed and resting. At nightfall they repeat the performance of transporting the aphids to the nests. Here is a circadian rhythm suited to the feeding of two different species!

DAYTIME FEEDERS

Of the insects active by day, honeybees are known for their extraordinarily keen sense of time. They tell time by the position of the sun. This sense leads them to a particular flower at the exact time it opens its petals offering a dinner of nectar. The story is told that a Swiss physician long ago discovered the honeybees' time sense when each morning during his breakfast the bees arrived to share his marmalade.

To test the honeybees' time sense, researchers in Paris carried out a series of experiments. They set up a feeding station where bees could come for a meal of sugar water. The dish was left for them at 10:00 in the morning and at noon. The honeybees always came at the appointed hours for their daily feed.

After a while, the experimenters transferred the feeding dish with sugar water to a room with the light on for 24 hours. But this time the dish was set out in the evening between 8:00 and 10:00. For some days the bees followed their schedule coming to the empty feeding station, still exploring the area in search for sugar. But after about a week they discovered that the schedule had been changed to the constantly lit room. They then began to arrive for dinner during the evening hours.

Later the same bees were flown at night from Paris to New York and placed in a similarly lighted room. Exactly 24 hours later they arrived to collect their meal during *their* accustomed hour. Only this time it was at 3:00 in the afternoon by New York time, 5 hours earlier by the clock. The bees didn't know what time it was, but their own inner clocks told them it was their dinner hour.

If honeybees dine according to the position of the sun and have an accurate time sense, one species of butterfly, the beautiful monarch, makes scheduled seasonal flights according to an inner "calendar." With the shortened day length in September, swarms of adult monarch butterflies are on the wing southward to spend the winter in California. These transcontinental commuters are not after food, but on the seasonal urge to reproduce. It starts with swarming when the butterflies mate. They spend the winter and, in March, return

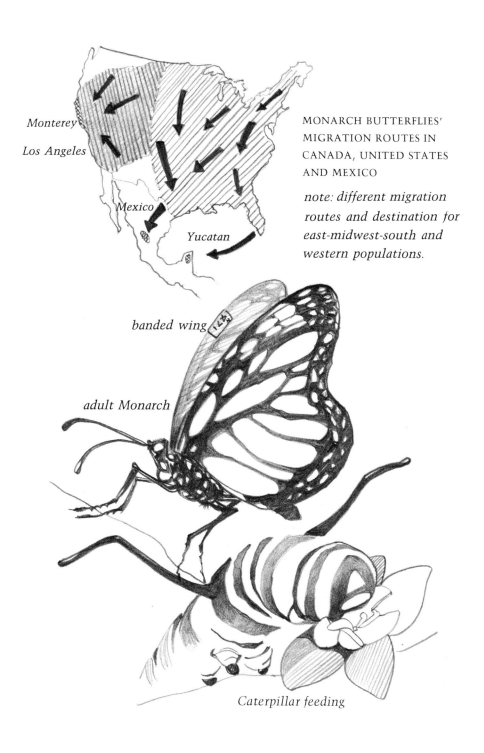

Monterey

Los Angeles

Mexico

Yucatan

MONARCH BUTTERFLIES'
MIGRATION ROUTES IN
CANADA, UNITED STATES
AND MEXICO

*note: different migration
routes and destination for
east-midwest-south and
western populations.*

banded wing

adult Monarch

Caterpillar feeding

home to the northern United States and Canada. The females then lay their eggs on the milkweed plant. In a few days the eggs hatch into larvae (caterpillars), which feed on milkweed. The larvae then enter the pupal stage and emerge as adult butterflies.

We value butterflies for their beauty and for their service in carrying the pollen to fertilize flowers. We depend on bees to make honey, and on ladybugs to rid the trees of plant lice. But the insects that destroy crops are a menace to truck farmers, fruit, grain, and cotton growers alike. Fortunately these agricultural workers now have ways to check the destruction.

BATTLING INSECT PESTS

Insect pests are controlled in different ways. They are sprayed with poisonous chemicals, lured by bait into traps, or attracted with light to instant death on electrified screens. Knowing the biological rhythms of insects helps agriculturists to cope with these pests.

For each species of insect there is a "best" time to spray with insecticides. Mosquito spraying is done after dark when mosquitos are most active. The chances of killing roaches and houseflies are best at 4:00 in the afternoon. The officer of the Department of Agriculture who discovered this in 1967 titled his report "Death in the Afternoon." Similarly it was learned that ten times as many boll weevils are destroyed by spraying three hours after daybreak than at sunrise.

In newer methods of dealing with insect pests the emphasis is not on killing by spraying the adult insects, but on preventing their becoming adults. This stops the breeding of a new generation. One such method has been used in the battle against the blackfly that has ravaged citrus trees in Florida. Certain wasps have been enlisted in this war. The wasps are released on blackfly-infested trees and lay their eggs among the blackfly eggs. The wasps' eggs hatch before the black-flies' do, so the wasp larvae eat the blackfly eggs. This cuts down the blackfly population. Of course, if the job is completed and there are no more blackflies in a certain grove, the wasps have to find another grove in which to lay their eggs. You can be sure it will be another grove with blackflies.

Another way to control pests depends upon knowing the photoperiod of an insect's stages of development. This was used with the cabbageworm, the larva of the white cabbage butterfly, which chews the cabbage leaves. It is known that the larvae go into diapause during the short days in the fall. Accordingly, lights were flashed on the cabbageworms at nightfall during this period. The worms were "fooled" into mistaking the light as the signal for wake-up time. The disrupted diapause ended the insects' winter hibernation. Their development was cut short, and they would not emerge in the spring. The farmer was thus rid of the pests for that year.

Another laboratory experiment revealed the boll weevil's habits of mating, information necessary for its control. The male produces a hormone called a pheromone that attracts the female. It was found that the insect releases 100 times as much of this sex attractant under a cycle of 16 hours of light and 8 hours of darkness than in total darkness. And the scientists also feed the caged insects certain poisons instead of freshly picked cotton buds to reduce the amount of pheromone produced by the males. Finally, the males can simply be made sterile by irradiation.

Here is how all this information was put to work to cut down the boll weevil population. First, the lights were manipulated to reduce the production of pheromone. When released into the field, the males could not attract the female. Second, the males were made sterile in the laboratory and released. Even when they were ready to mate they could not reproduce.

Knowing the life habits of different insect pests makes it possible to check their destructiveness by biological control methods. This cuts down the need for spraying with poisonous chemicals that pollute, harm people, and cost huge sums of money. Biological methods upset the insect rhythms and keep the pests from multiplying.

5

RHYTHMS IN COLD-BLOODED VERTEBRATES

COLD-BLOODED VERTEBRATES ARE backboned animals whose body temperature changes with the temperature of their surroundings. Reptiles such as alligators, lizards, snakes, and turtles are cold-blooded. Birds and mammals are warm-blooded, which means they maintain a constant body temperature in summer and winter, in the tropics and in the Arctic. Cold-blooded animals lack a built-in living "thermostat" to regulate their body temperature.

Alligators and crocodiles are amphibious; that is, they live part of the day in water and part on land. They move out of the water at sunrise and return to the water at sunset in a true circadian rhythm. In the daytime they are warmed by the sun. At night it is warmer in the water than on land. To stay warm they also spend more time on land in the summer and more time in the water in the winter. In other words, they are on long days in summer and on short days in winter. It is the way their timekeeping machinery regulates their life-sustaining rhythms.

A biologist wanted to know if he could change alligators' autumn schedule by keeping them in pens under artificial light longer than they would normally be in natural light. As he worded it, he wanted to see whether he could put them on their summer photoperiod. He conducted the following experiment.

In one pen he exposed alligators to an artificial sunrise by keeping the light on for an additional three hours. This made the day start sooner. In a second pen, "sunset" was delayed by three hours to make the day last longer. The temperature remained the same. It wasn't really summer or winter in the pens as alligators would find in nature. Only the day length was changed. What happened?

A few days after the light and dark cycle was changed artificially from autumn to the summer schedule, the alligators changed their behavior. In the first pen they moved out of the water earlier in the morning; in the second pen they returned later in the evening. They were reacting entirely to the change in the amount of light.

Alligators also follow a circannual rhythm in mating. This occurs in spring when the sun rises earlier. They mate in the early morning in the water and then move onto the land when the sun is still low.

EGG LAYING IN SEASON

A scientist looked into the egg-laying habits of a species of lizard that lives in southern California. The females of the fringe-toed sand lizards lay eggs from April through August. Day length touches off the clocks that regulate their reproduction.

Late in July, the experimenter placed two lizards in separate terraria that were filled with approximately

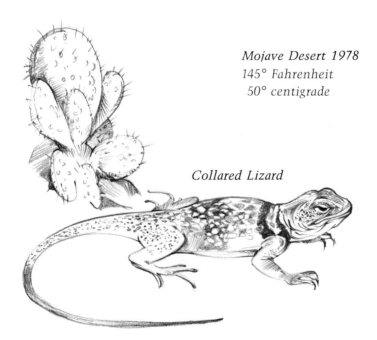

Mojave Desert 1978
145° Fahrenheit
50° centigrade

Collared Lizard

two inches of sand. The temperature in the terraria was kept at about 80 degrees, while the lights were kept on for 24 hours a day.

In November, when these lizards normally would be inactive under sand, they began to lay eggs. They continued laying eggs every four to seven weeks until February and March.

A third lizard that had been hibernating in an outdoor cage was placed in a terrarium at the end of November. Exposed to artificial light for 24 hours, it came out of hibernation and began to move and take food. The sides of its body took on a reddish-orange coloration, which meant the lizard was preparing to breed. In January it laid its first clutch of eggs. This was months earlier than it would have laid eggs in the field.

This experiment showed that light is more important than temperature for this lizard's breeding.

Timing In The Life Of Snakes

Land snakes mate in spring, lay their eggs in August, and in autumn crawl into burrows or under piles of straw and manure. There they remain until March or April. During their active season in summer they shed their skins all in one piece. Starting at the nose, the skin peels off the body like a stocking. Why do snakes shed them? They are casting off their upper skin layer

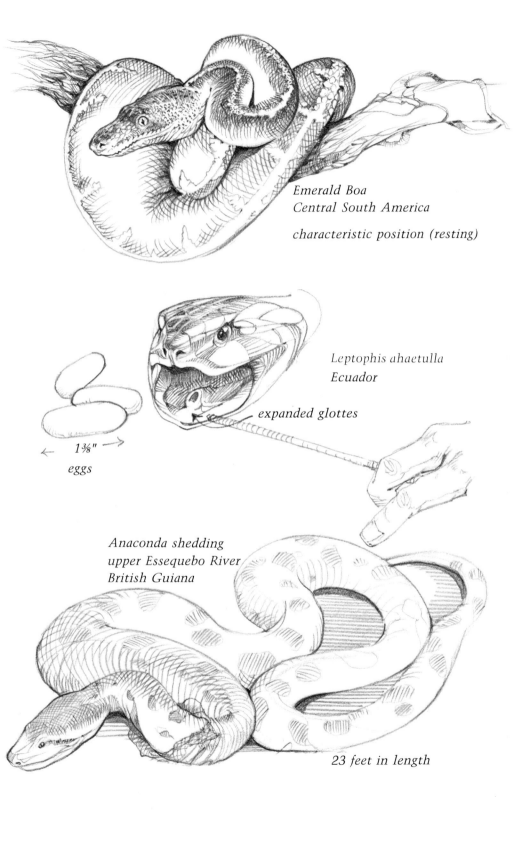

Emerald Boa
Central South America

characteristic position (resting)

Leptophis ahaetulla
Ecuador

expanded glottes

1⅜"
eggs

Anaconda shedding
upper Essequebo River
British Guiana

23 feet in length

just as humans do. Unlike us, they lose the skin all at once instead of some dead cells each day.

While the skin peeling occurs in the summer, when the snakes are active and growing, according to one snake expert, it is not so much due to growing as to eating. It depends upon the amount of food the snake takes in. A snake that feeds greedily sheds its skin more often than one that is not an eager feeder. Increased appetite and hearty eating are triggered by a hormone produced during the snake's active season.

A THOUSAND-MILE JOURNEY TO LAY EGGS

If sea turtles follow a daily rhythm of feeding and resting, we can only guess about it. We don't know what, when, and where in the brine they eat and sleep.

But more is known about the migrations of the mature females. Sea turtles are commuters on the high seas, journeying over a thousand miles from their feeding grounds to their nesting beaches. Green turtles have been tagged on Ascension Island in the Atlantic Ocean and later recovered on the coast of South America where they came to feed in lush pastures of turtle grass and eelgrass.

When the female green turtle is five or six years old, she is ready to reproduce. She leaves the water,

Green Turtles

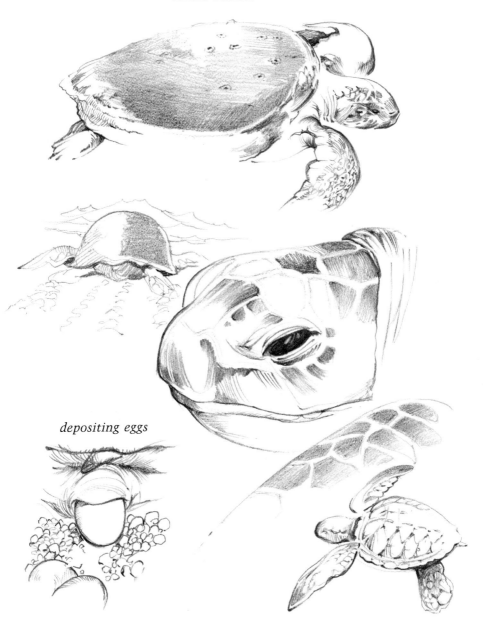

depositing eggs

small Pacific Green Turtle

coming to lay her eggs on the very beach where she was hatched. How she finds her direction to the same spot is one of the sea turtle's secrets still unbroken by scientists.

On Hutchinson Island in southern Florida, the egg-laying season for loggerhead turtles is from May to midsummer. In the evening on an open, quiet beach, the mother turtle emerges from the surf and slowly crawls up the beach. She finds a suitable spot well above the high-tide mark and digs a deep hole in the sand. One by one she drops over 100 eggs into this nest. Then she covers it with sand so carefully that most people could not find the spot. Exhausted from her labors, and having fulfilled her destined function to reproduce, the turtle trudges back down the beach to the sea.

Fifty-five days later each baby turtle cuts through the tough leathery shell with its "egg tooth." It is not really a tooth but a sharp point on the end of the snout. Together the dollar-sized hatchlings push up on the sand piled over them, opening the nest for their release. They then head for the sea and disappear in the surf. They are on the way to unknown feeding grounds. When they mature, their biological clocks will signal the time to return to the place where they were hatched. Like their parents they will complete their life cycle.

6

MANY
RHYTHMS
IN THE
WARM-BLOODED

MAMMALS ARE WARM-BLOODED. Their body temperature remains constant at about 100° F, the result of a delicate balancing of heat produced and heat lost. Mammals' biological clocks regulate when to feed, when to be active, and when to rest. There is a time to burrow, to stay out of a scorching sun, and to keep warm. Inner clocks signal the time for furbearers to grow thicker pelts for sleeping away the winter in a den. Others migrate to warmer climates with the coming of winter. There is a time for changing color, for mating, having babies, and nursing them through their helpless days.

A TIME FOR BABIES

Reproduction in mammals is seasonal, and the specific time of the year varies for each species. Short-day animals breed either in spring or fall, when there is less than 12 hours of daylight. Sheep, for example, breed in the fall. Rams (male sheep) and goats produce more sperm during short days. The ferret and the snowshoe rabbit breed in late spring when there are 14 to 15 hours of daylight. Raccoons, hares, white mice, and members of the furbearing weasel family, such as mink, sable, marten, and fisher, are also long-day animals.

Molting is a seasonal shedding of fur and starts with the lengthening day. It generally coincides with the time the animal becomes ready to mate. In animals of the weasel family, molting of the winter fur coat comes in late spring in cold climates. The process is triggered by the lengthening days of approaching summer. With the arrival of short days in the fall, these animals replace their summer coats by growing thick winter fur. In this way they prepare for survival during the severe cold in the north. A researcher exposed a silver fox, which had just completed its early summer molt, to an artificially short day. The fox began growing its thick pelt as if winter was on the way and it was preparing for the cold.

A TIME FOR WINTER SLEEP

Many mammals living in temperate climates face the

winter cold by taking a long snooze under cover. This could be in a cave, in a hollow or thicket, or in a dug-out der This seasonal suspension of activity is hibern:.ưon. The word comes from the Latin *hibernare,* meaning "to winter over." The shortening days of autumn signal severe weather and scarce food ahead. It is then time to prepare for winter.

About 20 years ago two researchers at the University of Toronto were studying hibernation of the golden-mantled ground squirrel under artificially arranged conditions. In its natural habitat this species is a seasonal hibernator. Just before winter sets in, its body temperature falls to 1 or 2 degrees above freezing, nearly 70 degrees below its normal temperature. Its heart slows to a couple of beats a minute, and its breath-

Golden-Mantled Ground Squirrel
(Citellus lateralis)

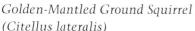

skull

statistics

8½—12¾ inches long
6–9¾ oz. weight
22 teeth

ing to perhaps only once a minute. It remains in this state through the winter months. One of these test squirrels was kept in a room without a window at 32° F for three summer months. The room was lighted artificially for 12 hours a day. Despite the freezing temperature of the air, the squirrel's body temperature remained constant at its normal summer level. It also ate when it wanted, and it continued to be active. On arrival of autumn in October, the squirrel stopped eating. Its temperature dropped to nearly freezing. The time for its winter sleep had arrived. No longer active, the animal lapsed into a stupor, just as it would have in natural hibernation. Six months later with the coming of spring, the squirrel came out of hibernation and became active once more. Its cycle of activity and hibernation was governed by the change in day length, not by the surrounding temperature.

Later, baby golden-mantled squirrels were raised in darkness from birth at a temperature of only 8 or 10 degrees above freezing. Despite these low temperatures and without light, they maintained rhythms of hibernation and activity for three years during which they were observed. They were born having the rhythms. There was however a difference: in the absence of seasonal light cues of day length, the rhythms were "free-running." The cycles were either longer or shorter than a calendar year.

The golden-mantled squirrel is one of many animals known as obligate hibernators; this means it enters a state of complete inactivity, taking no food through the entire winter. Another obligate or true hibernator is the woodchuck, commonly called the groundhog.

WOODCHUCK: A WEATHER FORECASTER?

By whichever name it is called, this hibernator's inner clock signals the time to prepare for a long winter underground. It digs a rambling den several feet deep, with an entrance at one end and an exit at the other. Long before food becomes scarce, the woodchuck eats ravenously all day through the summer. It doubles its weight and builds up a thick layer of body fat. By the fall it is ready to enter its den, prepared for hibernation.

All winter its body temperature is very low, its stored body fat burning very slowly as in a banked furnace. Its heartbeat and breathing are at the lowest rate that will sustain life. And during its hibernation it loses at least a third of its weight.

What brings the woodchuck into our story is its undeserved reputation for letting winter-weary people know whether spring is just around the corner or will be delayed. According to a centuries-old superstition, a certain event happens on February 2, celebrated as Groundhog Day, in Punxsutawney, Pennsylvania. On this day the animal supposedly emerges from its den to look for its shadow. If the groundhog sees its shadow in the snow, winter is not yet over. If it does not cast a shadow, spring is on the way. Newsmen, photographers, and tourists converge on the town to await the groundhog's seasonal forecast.

On this one day in the year the mountain folk in the quiet town enjoy national attention. But while the groundhog knows when to prepare for winter and when to leave the den by the amount of daylight, it does not follow our calendar. Science tells us that no woodchuck/groundhog would be so foolish as to leave the den before some time in March to check for its shadow, or for any other reason people have dreamed up.

Of other winter sleepers, bears, badgers, and raccoons are not true hibernators. Let's see what naturalists have found about the brown bear that they have tracked through the seasons.

The brown bear is not in a very deep sleep in winter. It may even sit up in its lair, and it can awaken enough to wander out for a bit. On occasion, if it comes upon a morsel to eat, it will not pass it up. The layer of fat it has in October or November will not last until March or April. When it leaves the lair in the spring, the bear will be much thinner.

Spring is also the time for mating. The bear is a short-day animal. The cubs will be born in the den the following December or January. During the remaining months of hibernation, the mother bear will suckle them. Together the adults and young will leave the

Pika gathering and storing grasses for winter

hibernating Chipmunk

Black Bear hibernating

lair, and the cubs will be cared for by the mother during the summer. In the fall, their own clocks will be touched off by the shortened day, signaling time for hibernation.

Some mammals do not hibernate at all. Living at high altitudes, caribou, mule deer, moose, and big mountain sheep roam all summer in the mountains. At the first snowfall, they just move to lower ground. Deer and moose are not furred animals, but they do have antlers that are renewed seasonally.

ANTLERS SHED AND REGROWN

In circannual rhythm, deer shed their old antlers during the mating season in the fall. In the spring they grow new ones, which is also the time when the fawns are born. Similar to molting in furbearing animals, the cyclic shedding and regrowing of antlers are related to mating, clocked by day length.

A biologist changed the time of shedding and growing of antlers in sika deer. He kept the animals indoors under artificial lighting and changed the day length to shorten the year to a "six-month year," a "4-month year," and even a "2-month year." What happened? Clocked by artificially changed day length, the deer replaced their antlers two, three, and four times during a 12-month year.

Other deer, which he kept under a cycle of 12 hours

CYCLE OF THE
GROWTH OF ANTLERS

Virginia Deer

of light and 12 hours of darkness, did not regrow antlers according to any regular rhythm. This type of yearly light cycle exists only at the equator. In the absence of the four seasons, deer that live at the equator do not have a regular mating time either. They shed their antlers and breed at any time of the year, and fawns may be born at any part of the year. This experiment again showed how the seasonal short and long days affect the life processes timed by biological clocks.

MIGRATING MAMMALS

Mammals that do not hibernate may migrate for the winter. Bats are the only flying mammals. Some bats hibernate in caves where they also mate and raise their young. Those bats that migrate to warmer climates breed in February and March, and the young are born when the lengthening days of late spring herald the time to fly back north.

Seals and whales, marine mammals who follow a circannual rhythm, migrate to southern waters to mate and bear young, returning north to their feeding grounds. The gray whales' seasonal migration is famous. Beginning in December they leave their home in the Bering Sea and swim southward, arriving by the end of February in the Mexican lagoons of Baja, California. Their arrival is as regular as the coming of the swallows of Capistrano. Sightseers travel thousands of miles to watch the parade of these magnificent mammals.

In the warm waters some whales mate; those that mated the previous year give birth to young. From March to May they head back to northern seas to fatten up, browsing along the way on small shrimplike animals called krill. Returning south the following year, they take no time to eat. They are propelled on that long journey by the urgent need to breed, just as the cold-blooded sea turtles suspend feeding to deposit their eggs on the ancestral beach. There are no more striking examples of biological rhythms than these cyclic, annual events of breeding and feeding, functions for the survival of a species.

PETS ON MASTER'S TIME

Are you wondering whether your pet dog or cat follows annual and daily rhythms that are guided by the changing season or day length? Remember, pets are domesticated. They eat when you feed them. Living in your home and not in the wild, their surroundings are artificially lighted, seasonally heated and cooled, as suits humans.

If your pet is a hamster, its rhythms would also be blurred. But in the laboratory, scientists have discovered that the hamster has a built-in, stable circadian rhythm. In wheel running, hamsters are long-day ani-

Hamsters

mals, active when exposed to more than 12.5 hours of light. Kept under a light for less than 12 hours, they slow down in their movements and the development of their sex organs is delayed. To reproduce they also require the seasonally long days.

What about nocturnal animals, such as rats and bats? Rats are awake and active at night. They also mate during the night. If the female is exposed to light two hours before she is ready to discharge the egg, she will not release it. The breeding of rats is stopped just by turning on the lights during the dark period of the cycle.

Bats are also nighttime mammals. They fly by night, feeding actively on those insects that are nocturnal. At daybreak they return to roost in caves, barns, or church bell towers.

So it is that for both diurnal and nocturnal animals, light of changing duration sets the clocks for activity, rest, and reproduction.

7

RHYTHMS
IN
THE
LIFE
OF
BIRDS

WHETHER THEY TAKE to the air in flight, dive into the water, or are landbound, all birds are warm-blooded. Their temperature is constant at about five degrees higher than mammals'. The word *bird* is thought to have come from the Old English *breden,* meaning "to cherish" or "to keep warm." Birds' eggs are hatched by the warmth of the parents' bodies.

If there are trees in your yard you may have noticed the daily rhythm of some common birds. Most birds are diurnal, awaking just before or at dawn. Some people are awakened early by their chirping. In feeding and roosting, birds are on a predictably circadian rhythm. During the day they seem to be eating all the time. In proportion to its weight, a bird eats more food than any other animal, including humans. It takes all that food to generate energy to maintain its body temperature and sustain the bird's almost continuous motion to get the food. A row of birds perched on a telegraph wire, the edge of a roof, or a tree limb, are taking a brief rest from feeding.

Nocturnal birds are also on a 24-hour schedule. The nighthawk, kiwi, woodcock, night heron, and nearly all owls are active at night. In the daytime they rest, and at dusk they take off to feed. Some fly after insects that are on the wing at night. The barn owl preys on mice and rats. The night heron finds fishing for food best at night.

By changing the number of hours of light and darkness it is possible to change birds' behavior. When diurnal birds kept in dim light were exposed for only 15 minutes to bright light, they became active earlier. When bright light was flashed on nocturnal birds they went to sleep, as if they would in the daytime. In nature, as the days grow longer in spring, nocturnal birds increasingly delay activity until darkness sets in, while diurnal birds awaken earlier each day.

CIRCANNUAL TIMETABLES

Birds are seasonally scheduled for molting, mating, displaying spring plumage, nest building, brooding (incu-

Short-Eared Owlets

Screech Owl

Great Gray Owl

Barn Owl

bating the eggs), caring for the young, and migrating yearly. Light is the time-giver for the biological clocks that govern these activities.

As the days shorten, diurnal birds are ready for a seasonal change. Winter is not far off, and food is becoming scarce. They are timed to prepare for migration to warm climates, where there will be plenty of food. Then as the days grow longer it will be time to fly home to breed. There they will shed winter feathers, and the males will display their brightly colored spring mating plumage. They will mate and build nests.

Birds take these regular migrations to the same place each year. In the fall, flocks of swallows and wild ducks, geese, cranes, and storks fly in formation from the Northern Hemisphere to their wintering sites. Do birds fly south because their food runs out? No, because they are often on their way when enough food is still available. For instance, the young bobolink,

Canada Geese in flight

Black-Chinned Hummingbird

male Canvasbacks

Brown Noddy Tern

hatched early in June, starts to fly south in August or early September. Yet there are plenty of grain seeds, caterpillars, and insects to be had. Having never done it before, how does a four-month-old fledgling "know" it is time to migrate? It must be that it hatched with a clock that "ticks off" the time of the approaching season.

The following experiment shows the part the amount of daylight plays in the timing. Juncos migrating south from Canada were captured in autumn and kept in aviaries at 32° F, the mean temperature in Canadian winters. The researcher turned on a few electric bulbs at sunset a little longer each evening. In this way he extended the length of day. By mid-December and with the temperature still at freezing, the birds were singing mating calls as they do in spring. And when they were then released in the dead of winter, the birds headed north instead of south. The light also triggered sexual development, and the birds had the urge to mate. They needed to return to their breeding grounds in the north.

Canada Goose

LOGGING THEIR TRAVELS

In their migrations birds travel at different times of the year, at varying speeds, and by special routes. They have been tracked in their flights by radar and by banded tags or rings on their feet.

Perching birds may travel at night, a time when they are better protected against birds of prey. Swallows fly by day, and nearly always with their mouths open to catch airborne insects. During the night they are likely to stop to rest in trees near swamps.

Birds migrate along definite routes called flyways. On the American continent, there are four major flyways within the four time zones: eastern, Mississippi, central, and western. The swallows of Capistrano come to nest in southern California, taking the western flyway on their way from Mexico or Brazil. The golden plover travels from northern Canada to Brazil and Argentina along the eastern flyway.

The longest travelers are the birds whose range of food is limited in their home territory. The Atlantic puffins return to Iceland during its brief summer to breed on island cliffs of volcanic peaks. Each female lays and incubates a single egg in a lava burrow. Then she abandons the young chick before it is fully fledged and takes off to feed in the ocean, the only place where she will find food. The chick meanwhile feeds on its own fat, but will eventually fly off to sea.

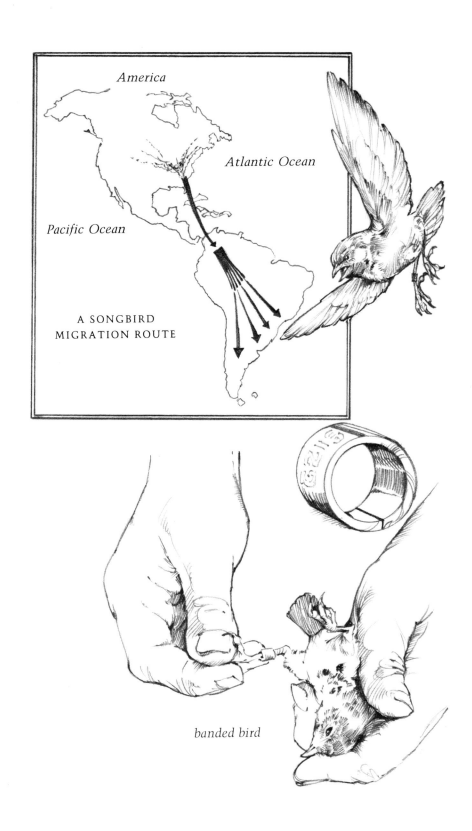

America

Atlantic Ocean

Pacific Ocean

A SONGBIRD
MIGRATION ROUTE

banded bird

The arctic tern summers in the Arctic and winters in the subantarctic. From June to August the terns nest in northern Europe, Asia, and Alaska. Between September and November they fly south to spend the southern summer (December to March) as "residents." On this round trip they cover 18,000 miles. Do they use the sun and stars to stay on course during their day and night flying? A partial answer came from observing another long-distance flyer, the indigo bunting. It breeds in northern Manitoba, Canada, and winters in Central America.

A group of indigo buntings were picked up in autumn and placed in an aviary under natural light. Another group was placed under advancing daylight, made artificially longer each day. By calendar spring, the birds under natural lighting showed changes of sexual maturation: molting and increased fat deposits. Shedding their feathers and replacing them with new ones, they were preparing for breeding. But the birds whose time schedule had been speeded up were already in condition for autumn.

Both groups of birds were tested in a planetarium in which the star pattern was like that of the spring sky. The group that had been under natural seasonal conditions turned northward for springtime breeding. The others, under premature autumn condition, headed south as if for winter migration.

Not all birds migrate. Some are permanent residents.

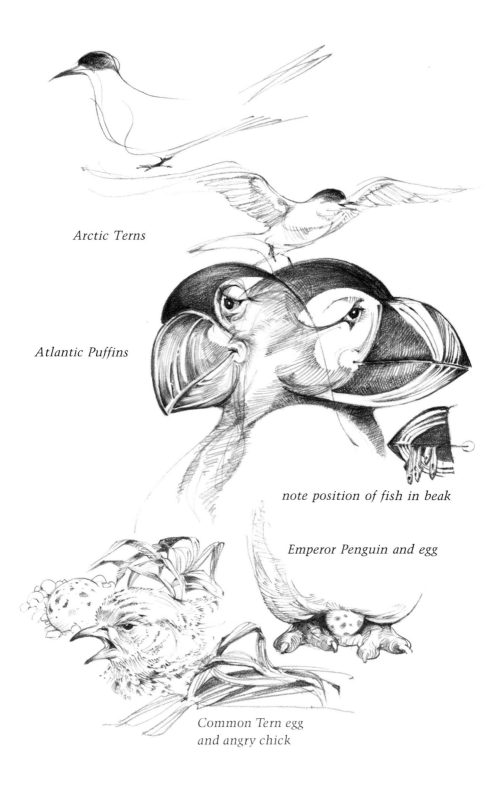

Arctic Terns

Atlantic Puffins

note position of fish in beak

Emperor Penguin and egg

Common Tern egg
and angry chick

The ring-necked pheasant, ruffed grouse, and bobwhite stay in the same place, feeding on grain and weed seeds, wild fruits, leaves, and occasional insects. Others, such as the sparrow hawk, feed on rodents, lizards, small birds, snakes, and poultry. All of these find plenty of food at home. So do the downy woodpeckers; they can find ants and boring insects the year round in their permanent residence. Their biological clocks remain stopped because the changing seasons do not reduce their food.

Ring-Necked Pheasant

Golden Pheasant

Birds That No Longer Fly

All penguins are seabirds. Their ancestors had wings and could fly, but living penguins have lost this ability. Their wings are short paddlelike flippers, suitable for swimming. They feed in the ocean and go on land in season to mate, to bear young, and to molt. The emperor penguin is the only one of the four Antarctic penguins that breeds in winter. In late March (southern fall) they make the long trek across the Antarctic ice on foot, sometimes tobogganing on their bellies. After penguins arrive at their breeding ground, male finds female and they mate. (But because there is no identifying change of plumage it may take two months for a male to find a female.) There is also no nest building because there are no materials available for making a nest.

As soon as the female has laid her single egg, the male starts incubating it. For two months he keeps the egg on his broad feet, under cover of a loose fold of belly skin like a blanket. He never eats and loses about half his weight before the chick hatches. In the meantime the female goes off to sea to fish. She returns in time to feed and care for the baby penguin.

A baby penguin, hatched in the southern spring (our autumn), is covered with a fluffy coat of down, a sort of mussed-up brown fur. It cannot swim, is fed around the clock and warmed by its parents' warmth. One or the other parent goes to sea to locate food, eats it, and returns to the baby penguin. After the food is digested, the babies suck the food out of the adults' mouths.

The young grow fat, molt, and grow the protective feathers that insulate them in the sea. After their first winter they are taught to swim. Surely biological clocks are timing these events. Emperor penguins are scheduled to mate in the hostile Antarctic winter, and the young are hatched in time for the approaching southern summer, the season for spending their infancy.

8

THE
TIMEKEEPER
IN
THE
BRAIN

IN THE BRAIN of all vertebrates there is a small gland. It has the shape of a tiny pinecone, which is how it got its name—pineal gland. In mammals, the pineal is hidden deep between the two halves of the brain. In lizards, the pineal sits closer to the top of the skull under the skin. In some lizards, the pineal has cells that react to light. But what does the pineal do in mammals, including humans?

Three centuries ago a famous French philosopher stated that images from the eye passed to the pineal by means of a "string." Receiving the message, the pineal then allowed "animal humors" (the ancient name for body fluids) to flow down hollow "tubes."

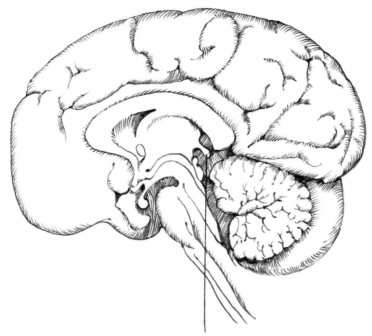

pineal gland

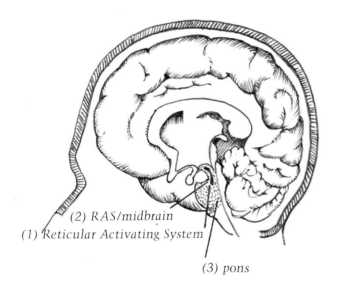

(2) *RAS/midbrain*
(1) *Reticular Activating System*

(3) *pons*

1. *Governs wakefulness and sleep*
2. *Controls deep and light sleep*
3. *Controls alertness*

In his day nerve fibers were thought to be narrow pipes. And as recently as our century, a celebrated American physiologist called the pineal a "museum piece" from a bygone era, as if it no longer had any use.

In the first decades of our century it was learned that a substance in the frog's pineal caused its dark skin to lighten. Then in 1959 this substance was discovered in the pineal of cattle. Finding it in a mammal sparked great interest in the pineal. And from the many studies that followed came the knowledge of what the pineal does. Here is some of what we now know.

The pineal gives the "right" time for sleep and wakefulness in mammals and for seasonal rhythms in birds and mammals. In sparrows and starlings the circadian rhythm of feeding and roosting is related to this substance. It delays the development of the ovaries and testes in rabbits, as well as children until puberty at about age 13 to 15. It controls the timing of menstrual cycles in mature females. What is this substance in the pineal? It was given the name *melatonin* for a reason. The dark pigment in the frog's skin cells is called melanin, which means "black." Melatonin from the pineal puckers up these cells, hiding the pigment and thus blanching the skin.

Melatonin production rises and falls in rhythm. It is made in the pineal from serotonin, a substance found in the brain, in the blood, and elsewhere in the body. The transformation of serotonin to melatonin and back again is the work of an enzyme found only in the pineal. (Enzymes are products of living cells that speed up and slow down many of the body's processes. They work in both directions, as in this case.) This enzyme is itself affected by light.

Under constant light, melatonin production is reduced, its activity declines, and the pineal gland shrinks in size. The reverse happens in darkness. When the pineal glands of rats were exposed to alternating 12 hours of light and darkness, melatonin showed a circadian rhythm, falling and rising alternately with light and dark. This is what happens also normally inside the body of the nocturnal animal.

In diurnal animals, the rise and fall of melatonin was in the reverse order. Thus in hens, the pineal glands produced more melatonin, and were heavier in the daytime when the hens were active than in darkness when they were roosting.

Apparently in timing light-dependent rhythmic activities, the pineal came to be considered the "master" clock. But how does light reach the pineal in mammals, since it is deeply buried in the center of the brain? The fact is light does not reach it, but its effects can be traced to the pineal in a roundabout way.

FROM THE EYE TO THE PINEAL

Light entering the eyes forms an image on both retinas. Nerve impulses from the stimulated retinas travel from the back of the eyes along nerves in a bundle called the optic tract. This is like a cable of nerve fibers, carrying messages to the sight center in the brain. However, a smaller bundle of nerves branches off from the main cable. It relays messages to a cluster of nerve cells elsewhere in the brain. From here nerve messages are carried to the pineal, "alerting" it to light and its duration.

If this cluster of nerve cells or the nerve fibers leading from it to the pineal are cut, the message to the time-keeper is interrupted. It is like the cutting of an electric wire or the pulling of the switch that shuts off the current from the light source.

THE TIMER AT WORK

The pineal carries out its timing through its connections with other parts of the brain, and does not directly influence the organs that work in rhythmic cycles. It sends nerve messages to a part of the brain called the hypothalamus, a center at the base of the brain. This center regulates body temperature, blood pressure, appetite, the use of sugar and fat by the tissues and, through its "drinking center," balances water intake and output. Responding to the pineal, the chief timer, the hypothalamus is like a lower-level biological clock.

The hypothalamus produces a number of releasing

hormones. These chemicals flow into the blood and reach the pituitary gland, located nearby in the brain. It too produces many hormones. One, for instance, controls the size of the pigment-containing cells in the frog's skin, changing it from dark to light. The pituitary secretes hormones to the ovaries and testes. The hormone to the ovaries prepares the egg cell for discharge; the one flowing to the testes causes them to produce sperm. In this way, the biological clock in the hypothalamus indirectly triggers sexual activity.

The pituitary also sends hormones to other glands, which, in turn, produce hormones of their own. Two little almond-shaped bodies, one on top of each kidney, are the adrenal glands. You may remember that at the moment of awaking, there is an outpouring of steroids, hormones that set you up for the day's activities. Steroids come from one part of the adrenals. Another part produces adrenaline. During exercise adrenaline races your heart, increases blood pressure, and rushes sugar from the liver into the blood.

TIMING OF SEASONAL RHYTHMS

The pineal times molting, migrations, changes in color and texture of fur. In spring, the weasel begins to show its brown fur as it gets ready to mate. At the same time the pineal signals the time for the pituitary to send its hormones to the gonads (ovaries and testes). It is time to discharge the egg and produce sperm. Then with shortened days in the fall, the weasel develops its winter coat of thick, white fur, and its gonads shrink to the size of their inactive period.

Chickens also "measure" day length by the pineal timekeeper. Egg laying is seasonal. With the waning light of autumn, egg laying falls off. To lay, hens need bright light for at least 13 hours a day; they have a long-day photoperiod. Poultrymen turn lights on in the hen house to extend the length of day in the fall. Chicken breeders often keep lights on at night for chicks in brooders, but for a different reason. The light keeps the chicks awake; they become active, keep feeding, and grow faster.

LACKING A PINEAL

What do animals that have no pineal do without a timer in the brain? The earthworm has neither a true brain nor eyes. Yet it follows a rhythm of nightly feeding and daytime resting in tunnels in the soil. Even without eyes, a worm is extremely sensitive to light through sense organs in its skin. Its nerve cords and a ganglion (a cluster of nerve cells) at the head end regulate its rhythmic movements. Its timer must be in its head ganglion.

The primitive sea slug, a mollusk without a shell, moves so slowly that we borrow the word *sluggish* from its name. With only a scattering of nerve cells, does it follow a circadian rhythm? A naturalist-photographer bent on finding out followed it around all day with a camera. When he speeded up the film to study its movements, he found that the slug was very active at dawn and again at dusk. The naturalist-photographer stimulated a single nerve cell. The speeded-up film picked up darting and jumping movements during the slug's active period.

In one-celled organisms, the biological clock is within the cell. A marine alga called mermaid's wineglass is a single-celled plant. Like all green plants it turns to the light in the daytime. Even when part of this giant cell, which contains the nucleus, was snipped off, the rest showed the photosynthetic (the plant's food-making) rhythm; it turned to a test light and away from it, alternately on and off.

The euglena is a one-celled animal and sports the green pigment of plants. You might say it leads a double life, both as plant and animal. In an unfailing daily rhythm, the euglena turned to the light in the daytime, but not at night.

Individual cells in many-celled animals also show rhythm. A rat's heart was kept beating by flushing it with a solution simulating blood. By means of a chemical "dissection," individual cells were separated out and kept in a dish bathed in the solution. The individual cells followed the rhythm the whole heart did during the course of a day.

Living clocks time the activities of the cells of plants and animals. The capacity for rhythm resides in each and every cell. In the complicated many-celled animals, the pineal acts as a kind of "internal manager," coordinating the circadian, tidal, lunar, and circannual rhythms.

9

BIOLOGICAL
RHYTHMS
IN
PEOPLE

WHAT ABOUT RHYTHMS in people? Is there always the same regular rhythm in your daily schedule? On the weekend or a holiday, you may sleep later than on school days. Or you must rise earlier to prepare for a trip. Animals cannot make such decisions to deviate from their normal natural timetable.

If your school happens to be on "split session," you may be assigned a lunch hour at 9:45 in the morning or at 1:30 in the afternoon. Either you are not ready for lunch so soon after breakfast, or your hunger has left you by the time of your assigned lunch. Your dinner hour in the evening will be at a time convenient for the family. It may not always be the time when your inner clock lets you know you are hungry.

We can consciously adjust our schedules of waking, working, eating, and sleeping. But within these artificial schedules we set for ourselves, there are scores of rhythms of which we are not conscious. We are not aware of increases of heart rate and breathing, of the hormones flowing into the blood when or just before we awaken, and of those that replace them in the night. We are not conscious of the different stages of digestion and the absorption of the products of digestion, nor of the casting off of wastes by the kidneys. The cells in the skin's upper layer (epidermis) are constantly dividing, and the dead cells are shed. This cell division goes on at a slower rate in the daytime than at night. So also bone marrow produces new blood cells to replace worn-out ones on a circadian rhythm. These and other body rhythms have been identified and recorded in chronobiology laboratories as regularly timed events. It is important to know not only what a person's normal blood sugar is, but also when it peaks and drops during a 24-hour period. Let's see how the daily rhythms work in health.

TRACKING RHYTHMS
IN A LABORATORY

Scientists have measured and charted circadian variations in the functions and behavior of healthy young

men at 3-hour intervals over a 72-hour period. All were
on the same schedule for rest and activity and for
meals. It was found that both body temperature and
pulse rate rose, peaked, and fell at about the same
rhythm. The men's performance in adding a column
of figures, counting fingers, and coordinating eye and
hand movements was best when the temperature and
pulse peaked. Vigor and mood were also highest when
the temperature and pulse were at their high point.

In another experiment the substances in blood and
urine were measured during hours of activity and rest.
Blood serum was tested for proteins, enzymes, glucose
(sugar), salts, and fats; urine was tested for acidity,
urea (waste from proteins), salts, steroid hormones,
and for total volume excreted in an hour.

It was found that the peak and trough values of
certain items are related to each other in time. For
example, the excretion of sodium and potassium follows the same rhythm very closely, and both are related
to the excretion of water.

Also in rhythm, the concentration of wastes in the
urine rises and falls. Water and salts are excreted first,
the wastes from protein metabolism later. And if a
drug has been taken, its disposal is timed to follow
the work of the liver to break it down.

These cycles continue for hours after we have experi-
enced the rhythm of hunger and the satisfying feeling
of "having had enough" after a meal. Each cycle in
turn is set off by thousands of biochemicals that flow

to nerve endings or in organs always at the right time and in the right amounts. This is what happens in a healthy person, but at times things go wrong.

STRESSFUL HAPPENINGS

Loss of sleep, worry, and stress cause the timing of cycles to be off. Even a slight shift in the rhythm may make you feel ill. This causes some people to break out in hives. Should you be offered food at such times, you may get indigestion. Persons allergic to pollen or dust have been known to react with greater discomfort to these irritants at a time of mental anguish. Such effects may disrupt normal rhythms more at certain times of day than at others.

Some effects of stress have been discovered in experimental animals. What has been learned in animals has been useful in the prevention and treatment of illness in people. It was found that animals are more susceptible to injury or even death at a particular period in the daily cycle. Rats exposed to very loud noise at the time when they are ready to begin their rest are thrown into convulsions. Alcohol, drugs, and poisons; chemicals that produce cancerous tumors; and radiation administered to rats at such times can be deadly. How do we know the period in the cycle of greatest risk? Discovery of the peaks of certain hormones in the rats' blood, for example, made it possible to predict how and when the animals would react most to stress, electric shock, or drugs.

In rats, certain adrenal hormones peaked just when darkness set in. Their blood clotted faster when the light was on at the end of the activity period. In the middle of the night it took one-and-a-half times as long to clot. Their immunity to infection by a virus or bacteria was greatest during the last hours of darkness, and lowest during the first hours of darkness. These times coincided with the peaks and troughs of immune bodies in the blood.

KNOWING PEOPLE'S NATURAL RHYTHMS

A rhythm of great regularity is the rise and fall of blood sugar during a 24-hour period. The blood sugar is low during the night, but it can fall at any time if we skip a meal or simply delay the dinner hour. At such times, people often become restless, irritable, quarrelsome, less efficient, and careless. Infants show their distress by crying when their blood sugar is low, even if by the clock they are not yet scheduled to be fed.

Population statistics provide evidence that other events are cyclic in the lives of humans. More babies are born between midnight and the early hours of the morning than at other times. The level of certain hormones in the mother's blood during those hours favors the birth process.

Coronary heart attacks are more frequent in the early morning. And more deaths from natural causes occur in sleep. People are diurnal, and nighttime is the low time in the cycle for blood sugar, body temperature, blood pressure, and the hormones that favor relaxation.

For most people the afternoon is the best time for such exacting work as radar operation, complicated mathematical computation, problem solving, and competitive tests. This is the time when the body temperature has reached its peak. In addition, our ability to know the time without the aid of a clock is best then. Gauging short intervals of time is also more accurate at the peak of body temperature. Students tested at the time of their normal peak temperature counted much faster and tapped a Morse key more speedily. Perhaps this is because the metabolism of the brain is higher at peak body temperature.

Still, not everyone's living clocks are set exactly alike. Some people awake at dawn. These early risers have been called larks, because they rise and shine, bursting with energy early in the morning. But when evening comes they say they "wilt and are ready to fold." Their body temperature and blood sugar rise earlier and faster in the morning, reaching a peak at nightfall.

The surgeon who doesn't operate in the morning because he says he can't open his eyes before 8:30 is brightest in the late afternoon and can work into the night. Such people are called owls. The clocks of larks and owls are set for different times of the 24-hour cycle, but their rhythms don't falter. Knowing your own rhythm could well help to find the best time for peak performance.

A DO-IT-YOURSELF MEASURE OF BODY RHYTHMS

The effect of biological rhythms on the performance of children in the course of a school day was studied by children themselves. The coordinator of the Talcott Mountain Science Center in Avon, Connecticut, adopted the method that had been introduced into some Minnesota high schools by Dr. Franz Halberg, a pioneer in chronobiology who coined the word *circadian* in 1959.

Dr. Donald P. La Salle, the director of the Connecticut school, set up his experiment to find out when was the best time of day for children to learn. In a laboratory-schoolroom 35 boys and girls, ranging in age from 10 to 16, recorded their temperature, pulse, blood pressure, greatest flow of air exhaled, speed in adding, eye-hand coordination, and handgrip strength. They made their entries six times a day, seven days a week for three months. In addition, they charted their mood and vigor, each on a scale of 1 to 7. Mood ranged from feeling "blue," usual state, more cheerful than usual, to "happy, elated." Vigor ranged from "inactive, tired," slightly more active than usual, to active and "full of pep."

Here is what was revealed in this project, nicknamed the fourth "R" (R for rhythm of the children's personal circadian profiles). About a third of the children turned out to be larks, the morning type; a third were owls, the afternoon or evening type; and another third were not especially of either type. An owl had the best physical performance, felt most active and cheerful in the afternoon, when temperature and pulse peaked. A lark had the opposite profile, peaking in the morning and lapsing in the afternoon.

As for the question of when was the best time of day to learn or teach certain skills in relation to each child's biological peak, the answer was surprisingly unexpected. What Dr. La Salle found was that "ironically, adding speed and vigor, as well as grip strength, mood, peak expiratory flow and oral temperature all peaked well in the afternoon hours . . . a time when most schoolchildren are on their way home from school or already at home."

Could you tell by how you feel, when you are most attentive and learn best, whether you are the morning or afternoon type? You probably could tell even without taking your temperature in the morning and evening.

CHRONOBIOLOGY IN THE SERVICE OF MEDICINE

Knowledge gained from this new science is perhaps most important for diagnosing disease and for treating sick people. In a hospital routine, time schedules are fixed. The doctor makes his rounds early in the morning. Medications are given on a schedule of three or four hours apart. Meals are served at definite hours for all patients on the schedule convenient for the hospital staff. In this routine no account is taken of biological rhythms. Yet, the very illness of the patient may have started with a change in the person's natural rhythm.

With chronobiology in mind, one doctor found that the same dose of a drug to reduce high blood pressure was far more effective at 6:00 in the evening and at midnight than at other times. Similarly, there is a best and a worst time to give chemotherapy treatment or radiation to cancer patients. It was learned from mice made sick with leukemia (a form of blood cancer) that they could be killed or "cured" with the same chemical depending on the hour when it was given. At 2:00 in the morning, 96 out of 100 mice died from the drug; only 4 out of 100 died on the same dose given at 8:00 in the morning or at 5:00 in the afternoon.

For cancer patients treated with chemicals or radiation, knowing the proper timing may mean the difference between improvement and failure. Knowing the circadian rhythm of the cancer cells, their peak rate of growth, could be a special dividend from chronobiology in treating patients. Perhaps, the best time to shrink a tumor would be the time when the cancer cells are vulnerable to drugs or radiation.

FREE-RUNNING RHYTHMS IN PEOPLE

Do humans alter their circadian rhythm under continuous light or darkness for an extended time? To find out, volunteers remained in isolation in caves for two and three months. Without realizing it some had extended their "day." One person lived a 24.8-hour day during the activity-sleep cycle. It happens that this is the exact period of the moon's rotation, the lunar day. For other individuals the cycle was either longer or shorter, but deviating from the 24-hour day. This is called a free-running circadian rhythm. It has also been observed in animal experiments.

Volunteers in the Laboratory of Human Chronophysiology at the Montefiore Hospital in New York live in isolation in a laboratory "apartment" for a week or more. Each person spends that time not in darkness, but is deprived of all time and social cues. The apartment, though complete in other ways, lacks windows, clocks, radio, TV. The volunteers have no way of knowing when it is day and when night.

Information is gathered from an electronic apparatus hooked up to the person with connections in the testing laboratory. Body temperature, pulse, blood pressure, volume of air breathed, and blood constituents are measured, recorded, and analyzed by a computer.

From the record of the changes in such persons cut loose from their accustomed social contact and timing of daily rhythms, it was found that there is a dissociation of circadian rhythm. A normal person who spent two weeks in such isolation was found to have a sleep-wake cycle longer than 24 hours. The time sense was also distorted. When asked how long the isolation lasted, the person said 12 days instead of 14 days actually spent in the apartment. The reason is he slept 12 times for more hours each time during the 14 days. In short the person was on a free-running circadian rhythm.

The pattern is different in persons with certain kinds of mental illness. For example, people who suffer from agitation bordering on mania tend to have rhythms that are running faster than normal. In depressed persons the rhythm is slower than normal. In treatment, a drug known to be helpful in the state of agitation slows the internal clock. In those who require stimulation, another type of drug speeds up the internal clock.

For patients with sleep problems, the knowledge gained from studying each individual in isolation from all time cues helps in diagnosis and treatment, as you will read in the next chapter.

10

RHYTHMS

IN

SLEEP

SLEEP IS AS regular a daily happening as the ocean tides. It has a compelling rhythm that we cannot ignore. People forced to stay awake in a wakeathon or those under torture in prisons find it easier to go without food than without sleep. Those who say they can go without sleep for days do not realize how often they fall asleep involuntarily for brief periods.

In sleep, the body restores itself. It is the time in the circadian cycle for repair of tissues and for growth in the young. The cells in the surface layer of the skin and in the lining of the mouth are more rapidly renewed during sleep than in waking hours. The same is true for cells in the cornea of the eye and in the hair follicles that push the hair out in growth.

During sleep, hormones circulating in the blood follow a cyclic rhythm. Beginning with the first hours of sleep, hormones are released from the pituitary gland. Among them is the growth hormone; another stimulates the part of the adrenal gland that produces cortisol, a steroid hormone. Near the time of awakening in the morning, cortisol is released into the blood. This is one of the hormones that prepares you for meeting the dawn of a new day. It is like a chemical "changing of the guard" from the sleep phase to the active phase in the circadian cycle. The body temperature then begins to rise, oxygen usage goes up, brain activity is increased. You are fully awake and ready for action! During the day, cortisol in the blood tapers off. By nighttime there is practically no more of it circulating, as if the system has shut down.

PRYING INTO A SLEEPER

There are also cyclic changes in the nature of sleep itself. More than a century ago, a scientist tried to find the peak time of deepest sleep, the time when only the loudest sound would arouse the sleeper. He never did find that single point of deepest sleep. We now know why. Sleep does not follow a smooth curve

from light to deep and then to light again. Instead there are stages of sleep, which are indicated as changes in brain waves (electrical) and in the movements of facial muscles.

In the early 1950s, a professor pioneering in the physiology of sleep and a graduate student at the University of Chicago followed brain-wave patterns in persons during nightlong sleep. In a sleep laboratory, student volunteers spent nights sleeping at their normal hours. Dangling wires leading from tiny electrodes placed on the top of the head, at the outer edge of each eyelid, and on the chin of the sleeper were plugged into an instrument. It recorded the sleeper's brain-wave pattern, movement of the eye, and tone (degree of tension) of the small muscles in the face, especially the chin.

The electrical pulses from these areas were transmitted to several levers that were each attached to an inked needle. Each needle swung up and down, writing strokes on a moving sheet of graph paper. Traced on the paper, the record showed the changes in the brain waves, when the eyes moved, when they remained still, and when the chin muscles contracted and slackened.

Twenty years and many thousands of volunteers later, such tracings in sleep laboratories have revealed that a sleeping person goes through several levels of sleep during four to six complete cycles. What may appear to you and me as odd squiggles on the tracing paper tell the researcher a great deal about what is happening in the sleeper. Is the person drifting into a deep sleep or moving into a low level of consciousness during minutes of dreaming? Is the person having a nightmare? Is he about to talk in his sleep or grind his teeth?

Infants also go through cycles of sleep, each lasting about 50 minutes. The outward signs of these cycles are alternating fast and slow breathing, movements of the head and eyelids, and suckling movements of the lips. These movements accompany stomach contractions, signals of coming arousal by hunger. With increasing age the cycles last longer, up to about 90 minutes in adulthood. Animals show such cycles that differ in duration in each species.

During certain stages of sleep *R*apid *E*ye *M*ovements are observed. This is known as REM sleep. Then comes a non-REM (NREM) period. The average length of a REM-NREM cycle is about 70 to 90 minutes, and the cycle recurs at regular intervals, usually four to six times during the night.

REM sleep has been studied especially in relation to dreaming. All people dream, and many times during the night. If a person is awakened at the time of REM sleep, the dream will be recalled perhaps three-fourths of the time. Since memory of a dream vanishes quickly, the awakening must be quick and the person immediately asked what is remembered of the dream. Some dreams last only a few seconds, and some people don't remember their dreams at all.

REM sleep seems to be important to the restoration process. If sleeping persons are wakened frequently during REM time, they show signs of being deprived of it, even if they are allowed to return to sleep. If they don't make up the time of REM sleep they are likely to become irritable or even fearful.

In persons who have problems falling asleep, who wake up frequently during the night, or who wake up before fully rested, the sleep rhythm is disordered, and the brain-wave pattern shows rapid, steep, spiked waves in stages not seen in normal sleep.

MANAGING SLEEP PROBLEMS

A patient with sleep problems who comes to a chronobiological laboratory seeks help. Doctors first study the patient to establish a profile: the brain-wave pattern, stages of sleep, including REM sleep. The hormones in their blood are measured as these rise and fall. While the patient in the isolation apartment has his sleep monitored, a small catheter (tube) previously inserted into a vein permits the collection of a blood sample at intervals. The information gathered about the hormones and other blood constituents measured helps the doctors find out the nature of the sleep problem. Next comes the decision on how to treat it.

Among the patients who have come to the Sleep-Wake Disorders Center of Montefiore Hospital and Medical Center in New York City, 10 percent were described as "night people." Theirs was not an inability to fall asleep, but rather to fall asleep at the right times. They would lie awake most of the night, sleep in the subway on the way to work, and doze off on the job. On weekends they slept most of the day, and they had a fear of being overcome with sleep while driving. Dr. Elliot D. Weitzman diagnosed this out-of-sync or offbeat rhythm as a "delayed-sleep-phase syndrome . . . a disorder of circadian pacemaking."

Instead of prescribing sleeping pills to cure patients of this condition, doctors were able to reset the pacesetter. This is how it is worked. The patient's bedtime is put off by 3 hours every day of a week. The patient is instructed to set his watch back by 3 hours, so that arriving home at 6:00 actual time, it is 3:00 for the patient by his watch. This delays his bedtime, say from 11:00 P.M. to 2:00 A.M. After sleeping for 8 hours the patient would then be about to wake at 10:00 in the morning when it is really 7:00. By delaying the bedtime 3 hours each "night," he is on a 27-hour day for a week. At the end of that week he has "added" 3 times 7 or 21 hours. But he has not really, for by then, he is back on a 24-hour day/week, and his watch shows the same time as everybody else's clock. This resets his sleep-wake schedule so that it is in keeping with the rest of the world. The treatment has proved successful, using the element of *time* as a means to cure the problem.

ON A MOONLIT NIGHT

Are humans affected by the moon? Those who believe we are reason that since we are four-fifths water, the pull of the moon draws us toward it. This tidal pull is supposed to be strongest at full moon, when it affects our feelings and behavior. Some people report that their sleep is disturbed. Others say they experience head-aches on the nights of the full moon.

The Navajo Indians believe that more babies are born at full moon than at any other time.

Some psychiatrists tell us that mood swings and ag-gression are related to the phases of the moon, espe-cially when the tides are highest. People suffering a condition of alternating mental depression and agita-tion complain that these problems are worse on those nights, and that their prescribed medication isn't work-ing.

Police officials claim that violent acts of crime, sui-cides, and traffic accidents peak on the nights of the new and full moon.

People like to think a moonlit night inspires lovers. A person is said to be moonstruck, madly in love, mooning, or sometimes even crazed.

Is there any truth to the Navajo belief? Does the moon really exert an extra pull on the fluid in which the unborn baby floats?

A physician-investigator attempted to get an answer. He checked the hospital records in New York City where 500,000 babies were born during three years. He found that the difference between the average num-ber of births during the first and second half of the moon's cycle was 1.01 percent. Although the average difference was slight, it indicated that the peak birth-rate was at full moon.

At another time and in another city hospital, the psychiatric staff tried to get an answer to the effect of the moon's phases on mental disturbances. The residents kept a record on nightly happenings in the psychiatric emergency service. Were there more persons brought in by the police on certain nights than on others? And were more patients themselves seeking psychiatric help during nights with a full moon?

If moonlight does indeed have such effects on some people, this did not show up in a sufficient number of cases in this study to prove it. Since many people hold such beliefs and some psychiatrists are studying this in their practice, we may someday get a reliably scientific answer one way or the other.

11

WHEN
BIOLOGICAL
CLOCKS
NEED
RESETTING

IN AN INDUSTRIAL society, work goes on around the clock. Telephone operators, flight-control personnel, nurses, medical interns, railroad workers, policemen, firemen, truck drivers—all who work at night reverse sleep and waking hours. But by circadian rhythm, the body is set for rest during the night. The activity of the nervous system is at its ebb phase. Body temperature and blood pressure are at their low points. For night workers, the cyclic flow of hormones is turned upside down.

People working other than what are biologically normal working hours find themselves out of step with family and society for their meals, leisure activity, and entertainment. All these are scheduled for the needs of the daytime world. Even when people learn to adjust to these inconveniences, there are real threats to their health. Night workers are known to be more prone to infection and poisons as well as to behavioral and mental disorders. Between two and four o'clock in the morning more errors are made in operations requiring concentration; there are more industrial accidents during those hours. To reduce these hazards and for better health, night workers have to have scheduled rests to break the routine.

Still greater havoc is caused by the rotation of shifts after some weeks of adjustment to the night schedule. In fact, some taxi drivers, policemen, firemen, and others object to changes of duty time. They prefer to remain on one schedule. Required to rotate often they are more likely to suffer from ulcers, hypertension, loss of appetite, insomnia, headaches, shortness of breath.

SPEEDING OVER TIME ZONES

In 1931, Willey Post, a U.S. aviator, and Harold Gatty flew around the world in eighty days. They were the first to recognize the effects of rapid crossing of time zones on sleep and work patterns. Today the millions

of persons who cross the continents and oceans in jet planes at 600 miles an hour know what jet lag means.

Traveling from New York to San Francisco a person crosses 3 time zones from eastern over central, mountain, to western clock time. Starting from New York at 1:00 P.M., one arrives after a five-hour flight at 3:00 P.M. in California, when the traveler's watch reads 6:00 P.M. Making the trip in winter, it would be dark in New York, but still light in California. Going from New York to New Delhi, India, crossing 12 time zones, means a complete reversal of a day's cycle. These rapid time changes over many time zones temporarily throw off the biological time clocks. Neither the brain nor the body has yet adjusted to the new day-night cycle.

The traveler is either sleepy or awake at the wrong time in relation to local time. Head clocks, stomach clocks, and elimination systems are disordered. The condition is called circadian dysrhythmia or desynchronization. Persons commonly experience confusion, loss of appetite, fatigue, and other upsets.

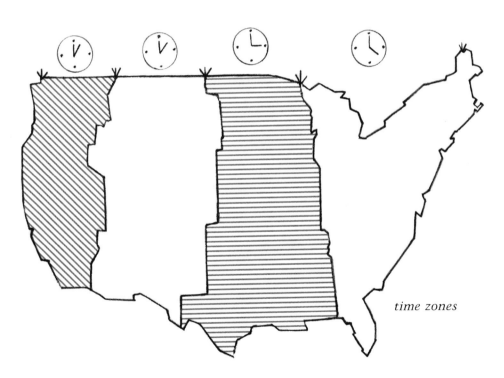

time zones

PREPARE FOR JET LAG

There is no cure for jet lag, but it is possible to lessen its effects, both before leaving on a trip and afterward.

1. Avoid losing sleep before leaving. Don't become exhausted before you start your journey. Without last minute dashing to the airport, allow enough time to attend to the details of checking in and locating your departure gate.

2. Wear comfortable, loose-fitting clothes. Remove your shoes as soon as you are seated. Your feet tend to swell on long flights at high altitudes.

3. To maintain good circulation, walk around at times when the Fasten Seat Belts sign is off. While in your seat go through circular motions of hands and of head and neck.

4. Try not to overeat. But drink lots of liquids—water, juices, or tea—as often as offered to prevent dehydration, a minor hazard in the pressurized cabin at high altitudes.

5. Before landing wash your face with cold water, freshen up, and take your time deplaning, especially if you have brought too much carryon luggage.

6. Most important, if you are touring, don't rush into sightseeing or shopping, but ease into your itinerary gradually.

And as you reset your watch to local time, remember that your biological clock also needs resetting. It takes much longer to adjust your body clock.

Persons traveling on business assignments, to attend international conferences or high-level government meetings take time to prepare themselves for their weighty duties. They plan to arrive at their destination on the weekend or a day or two before their appointment. Not everyone can do that, so there is another way to ease the adjustment to the new time: if you are traveling in an easterly direction go to bed an hour earlier each of several nights. Going westward, reverse the procedure, retiring an hour later.

Soldiers flying to Germany were prepared in still another way. A battalion of men from a military base in Texas were given anti–jet lag treatment. The men had a very light breakfast, omitting tea and coffee, which affect the body clock. Soon after lift-off, the soldiers were told to advance their watches by six hours to German time. They were served lunch, which was called supper. Lights-out was ordered at 11:00 P.M. on their watches, though it was 5:00 P.M. Texas time. Awakened five hours later the men were served a hearty breakfast that did not exclude coffee. The reset watches said 4:00 A.M., and the plane was due in Germany two hours later.

For the next five days the men's temperatures were taken every four hours; they were checked for their performance, sleep, and signs of fatigue. Compared with another crew that had not received this anti–jet lag treatment, they weathered the turning of night into day with no ill effects.

TRAVEL BY SEA

People traveling by modern ocean liners also cross time zones, but at a slower rate. The ship's time is changed by one hour each day as the ship crosses five time zones. Even this slower time change has some effect on passengers. The crew reports that more and more passengers arrive late for breakfast after the halfway point in the crossing.

If you are traveling to Australia or New Zealand, expect to have jet lag more so when going from eastern than western United States; you are crossing three more time zones. By the time you reach Australia you will have crossed the international date line, about the middle of the Pacific Ocean, and will have "lost" a day.

You will also have crossed the equator and gone through a change of seasons, say from summer to southern winter. What makes the change of seasons? The earth in its revolution around the sun tilts at an angle of 23.5 degrees from the plane of its orbit. So each hemisphere tilts toward the sun during half the year.

Leaving in summer you would be arriving during the winter; the reverse, if you were to take the trip in winter. However, you will need only a change of wardrobe. Your biological clock is not affected by the north-south trip. Only the crossing of time zones gives you jet lag.

Similarly birds migrating from the Northern to the Southern Hemisphere and back do not have a jet lag problem, and not only because they fly at a slower rate than a jet plane. Remember, they rarely cross more than one zone, as they stay in the accustomed flyways. If to avoid storms or high mountains, they do cross a time zone, they usually make rest stops. That takes care of any necessary adjustments.

But if birds are not traveling under their "own steam" and like mammals are shipped from their native lands to zoos over a number of time zones, they must make adjustments just as people do. On their arrival they are not ready for the zoo's human visitors. They are too sleepy or disorganized to be inquisitive about their new surroundings, as trained zoo keepers well know. They give the new arrivals time to adjust their inner clocks.

SUMMARY

WE LEARN THAT jet travel throws off our circadian rhythms, in sleep, and that daytime hormones are released into the blood as we awake, and replaced by nighttime hormones as in sleep. Chronobiology studies show there is a best time for medical treatment to avoid failure and bring improvement. Unborn babies have their kicking and quiet periods in cycles as mothers well know, and we work better in school at peak hours of the day, each at his or her own time of day.

While as conscious beings we can modify and even disrupt our circadian rhythms, we nonetheless find our 24-hour cycle shortened or lengthened without our awareness, as demonstrated by free-running rhythms in individuals established under constant illumination or darkness, without clocks, TV, or radio.

In plants and animals the rhythms are more reliably predictable. In the fall, Canada geese fly south on schedule, the woodchuck takes to its den for the winter, and the monarch butterfly migrates to California. Desert plants bloom with the seasonal rains, and arctic flowers during the two summer months of nearly 24-hour sunlight. Oysters open their shells with the flow tide, and the fiddler crab changes color in circadian rhythm. Alligators climb on land in the morning and return to their waterholes in the evening, spending more time on land in summer and more in the water in winter. Deer grow antlers in the fall and shed them in the spring; hens lay eggs in summer and abstain in winter. Bats fly by night in search of insects and sleep in caves in the daytime.

These are among the rhythms with which we and other living things are born. They are timed by inner living clocks.

FOR FURTHER READING

Brady, John, *Biological Clocks*. Baltimore: University Park Press, 1979.

Lieber, M. D., Arnold L. Produced by Jerome Engel. *The Lunar Effect. Biological Tides and Human Emotions*. Garden City, N.Y.: Anchor Press, Doubleday, 1978.

Luce, Gay Gaer. *Biological Rhythms in Human & Animal Physiology* (Originally published by the U.S. Department of Health, Education, and Welfare and the National Institute of Mental Health in 1970 as Public Health Service Publication No. 2088, under the title *Biological Rhythms in Psychiatry in Psychiatry and Medicine*). New York: Dover Publications, Inc., 1971.

*Moore, Shirley. *Biological Clocks and Patterns*. New York: Criterion Books, 1967.

Palmer, John D. *An Introduction to Biological Rhythms*. New York: Academic Press, 1976.

Palmer, John D. *Biological Rhythms and Living Clocks*. Edited by J. J. Head. Burlington, North Carolina: Carolina Biological Supply Company, 1977.

---

* Out of Print, but may be available in public libraries. It is a good little book; however, understandably out of date.

INDEX

ladybugs, 28, 34
larvae, 29, 30
La Salle, Donald P., 85, 86
learning, biological rhythms
    and, 85–87
light, 6, 9–10
    see also photoperiods
Linnaeus, Carolus, 11–12
lizards, 70
    collared, *40*
    fringe-toed sand, 39–40
lunar rhythm, 4, 18

mammals, *see* warm-blooded
    vertebrates
maples, sugar, 8
medicine, 87–88
melatonin, 72–73
mental illness, 89–90
mermaid's wineglass, 77
metabolism, biological
    rhythms and, 80–82
migration, 4
    of bats, 54
    of birds, 60–65, *64*, 107
    of gray whales, 54–55
    of monarch butterflies,
        32–34
    photoperiods and, 54–55,
        60, 62
    pineal gland and, 72, 75
    of seals, 54
    of sea turtles, 42
mites, velvet, *15*
molting, 46
    pineal gland and, 75–76

monarch butterflies, 32–34,
    33
moods, 2, 5, 81
moon, 2, 4, 18, 88
    birthrates and, 98–99
    crime and, 98
    feelings and behavior af-
        fected by, 97–99
    mental disturbances and,
        98, 99
    reproduction timing and,
        26, 27
    sleep affected by, 98
moose, 52
mosquitoes, 34

neap tide, 18
nectar, 14
"night people," 96–97
night workers, 100–101
NREM sleep, 95

optic tract, 74
owls, 2, 4, 58
    barn, 58, *59*
    great gray, *59*
    screech, *59*
    short-eared, *59*
oysters, 2, 20–21
    experiment with, 20

penguins, emperor, *66*, 68–
    69
pets, 55–56
pheasants
    golden, *67*
    ring-necked, 67, *67*